This flesh eating dinosaur lived and hunted in North America about 150 million years ago. It reached a length of 10 metres and stood 3 metres high. [...] million years, of the ev[...]

For more informa[...]

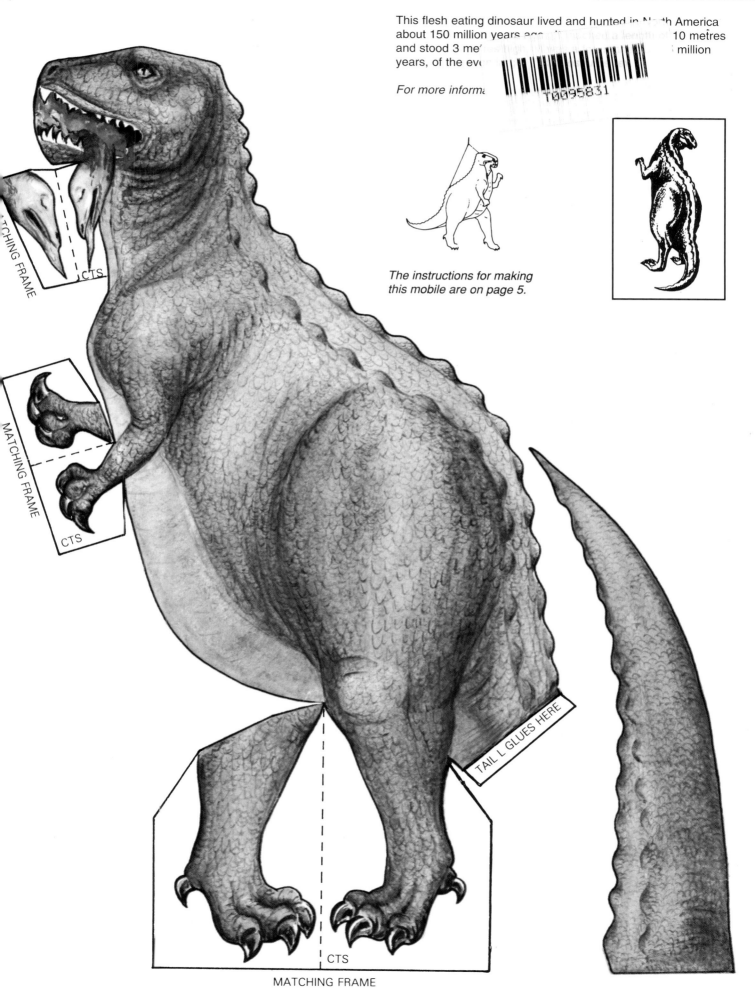

The instructions for making this mobile are on page 5.

MATCHING FRAME

CTS

MATCHING FRAME

CTS

TAIL L GLUES HERE

CTS

MATCHING FRAME

TAIL L

ALLOSAURUS

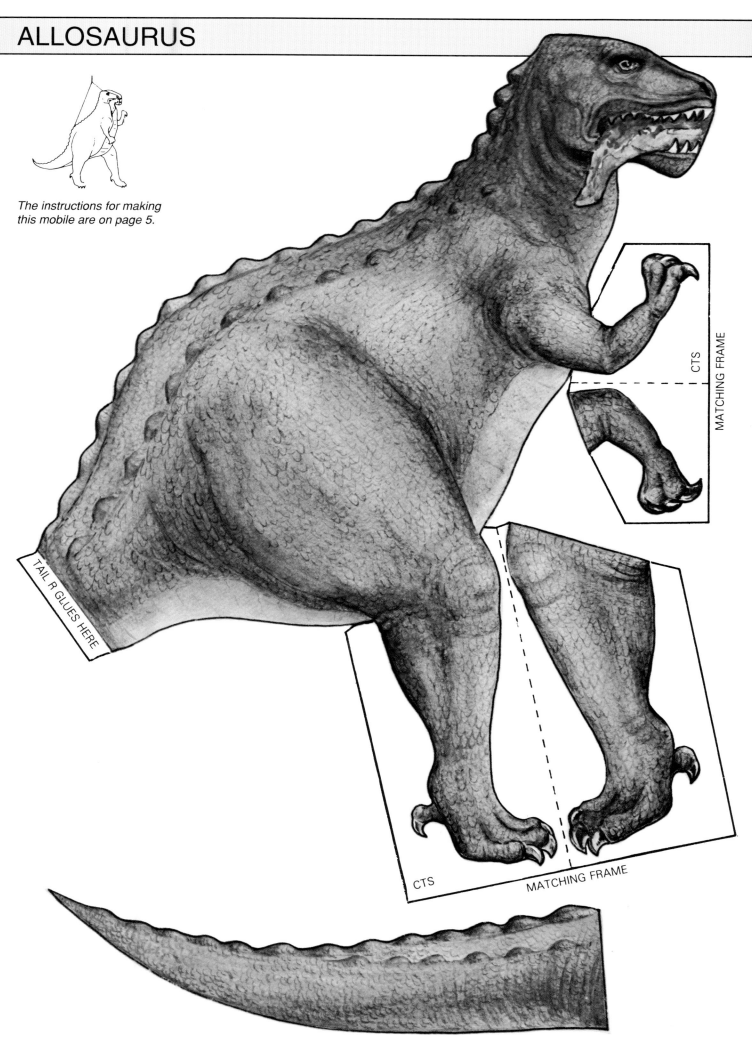

The instructions for making this mobile are on page 5.

CTS

MATCHING FRAME

TAIL R GLUES HERE

CTS

MATCHING FRAME

TAIL R

UNDERBODY/HEAD STRIP

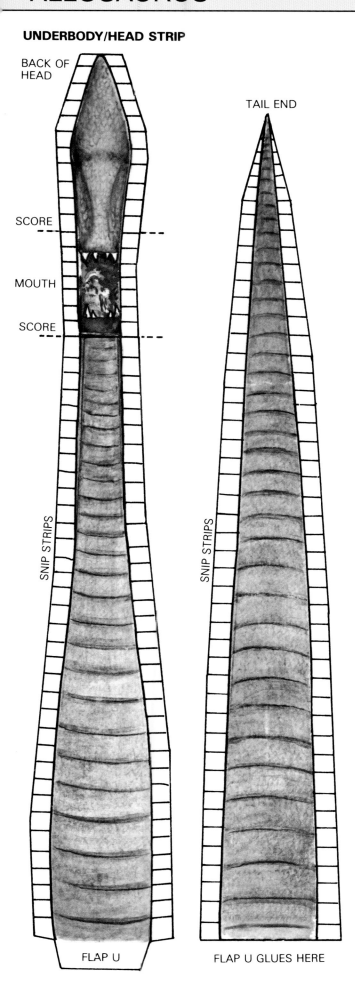

BACK OF HEAD

SCORE

MOUTH

SCORE

SNIP STRIPS

FLAP U

TAIL END

SNIP STRIPS

FLAP U GLUES HERE

To hang your Allosaurus mobile, use two threads as shown in this sketch.

HOW TO MAKE THIS MOBILE

1. Cut out the pieces on pages 1, 3 and 5 following the general instructions inside the front cover about scoring, cutting, matching frames and snip-strips.
2. Complete the two sides of the body by glueing the tails L and R to their corresponding flaps.
3. Complete the underbody/head strip by joining the two sections together.
4. Glue the underbody/head strip to the right side of the body by glueing a few "teeth" at a time. Start at the head end by first lining up the mouth. Complete the head and then work towards the tail.
5. Glue the left side of the body to the underbody/head strip in the same way.
6. Glue a narrow band along the back, pinching firmly together. Start at the head end and work towards the tail.

FLAP U
GLUES HERE

This dinosaur is easily recognised by the double row of plates along its back. They could have been a protective armour, but it is more likely that they were radiators, allowing the cold blooded creature to gain or lose heat when necessary. It lived in North America about 150 million years ago.

For more information see the minibook.

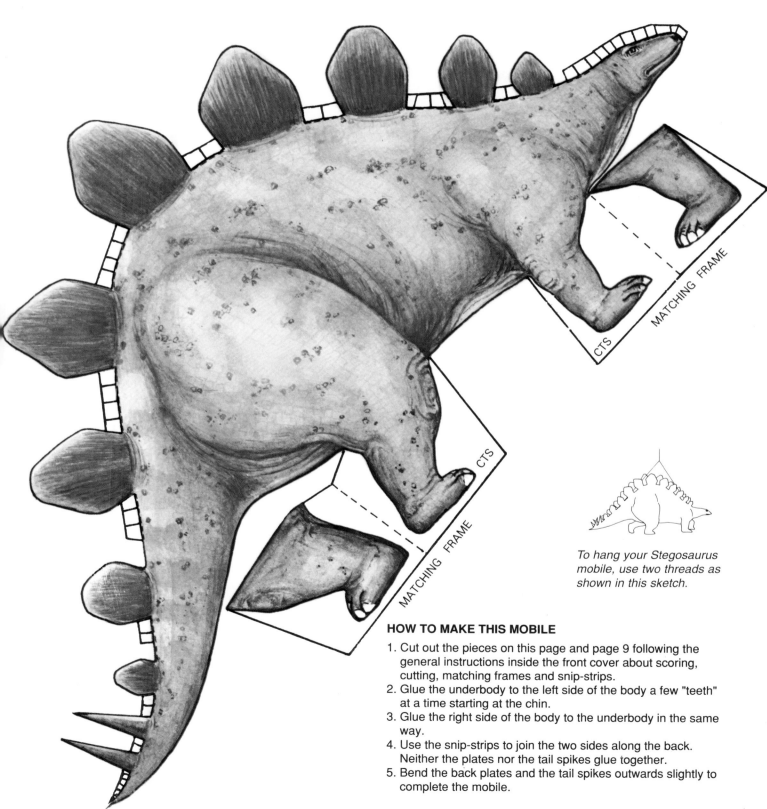

To hang your Stegosaurus mobile, use two threads as shown in this sketch.

HOW TO MAKE THIS MOBILE

1. Cut out the pieces on this page and page 9 following the general instructions inside the front cover about scoring, cutting, matching frames and snip-strips.
2. Glue the underbody to the left side of the body a few "teeth" at a time starting at the chin.
3. Glue the right side of the body to the underbody in the same way.
4. Use the snip-strips to join the two sides along the back. Neither the plates nor the tail spikes glue together.
5. Bend the back plates and the tail spikes outwards slightly to complete the mobile.

STEGOSAURUS

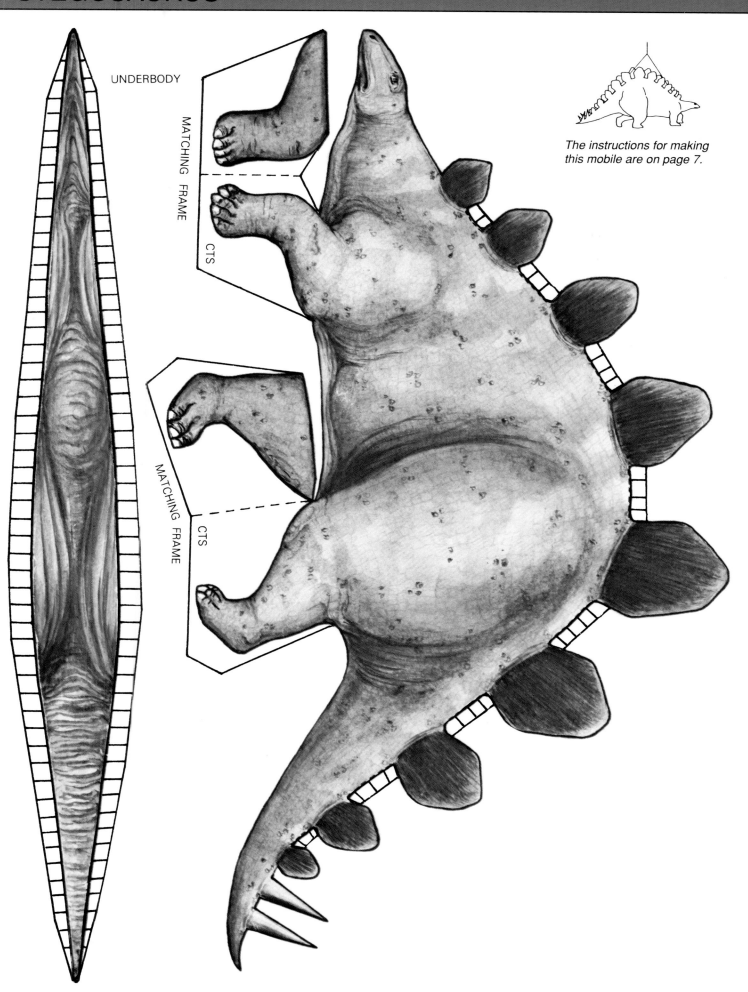

UNDERBODY

MATCHING FRAME

CTS

MATCHING FRAME

CTS

The instructions for making this mobile are on page 7.

HEAD END

TAIL END

This dinosaur lived in North America about 150 million years ago. Although its height reached 5 metres and its length up to 20 metres, it had a very small head, equipped with peg-like raking teeth for gathering the huge quantity of plants it needed to eat. It swallowed stones to help break down the plants in its stomach.

For more information see the minibook.

To hang your Apatosaurus mobile, use two threads as shown in this sketch.

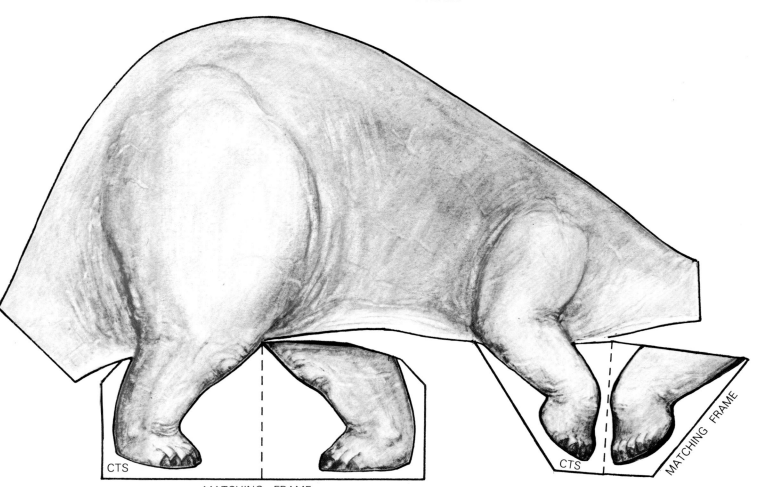

CTS

MATCHING FRAME

CTS

MATCHING FRAME

HOW TO MAKE THIS MOBILE

1. Cut out the pieces on this page and on pages 13 and 15, following the general instructions inside the front cover about scoring, cutting, matching frames and snip-strips.
2. Join the underbody to the left side glueing a few "teeth" at a time, starting at the head. The slight overlaps at each end tuck in afterwards.
3. Join the underbody to the right side in the same way.
4. Join along the back by glueing the snip-strips a few teeth at a time. Start at the head end.
5. Then follow the instructions for the pleated folding of the neck and tail.

a. First glue the two sections of the tail together making sure that you have scored the central line.
b. Then fold as shown, the top of each fold coming halfway up the previous one.
c. Then fold along the central line and by pinching the "spine" and gently pulling, ease it into a gentle curve.
d. Complete the neck in the same way. The two extra score lines mean that the neck has a fuller shape
e. Glue the neck and tail to the body and then ease into a natural shape.

APATOSAURUS

Fossilised footprints of *Apatosaurus* have been found, and from them scientists have been able to work out that they were capable of a speed of 2 mph.

For more information see the minibook.

The instructions for making this mobile are on page 11.

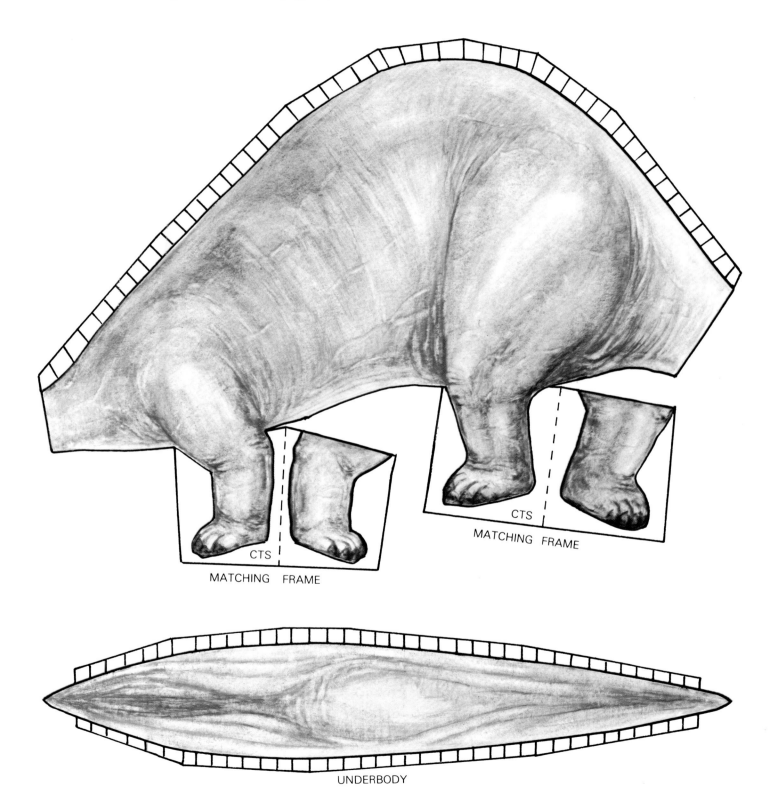

CTS

MATCHING FRAME

CTS

MATCHING FRAME

UNDERBODY

TAIL END   HEAD END

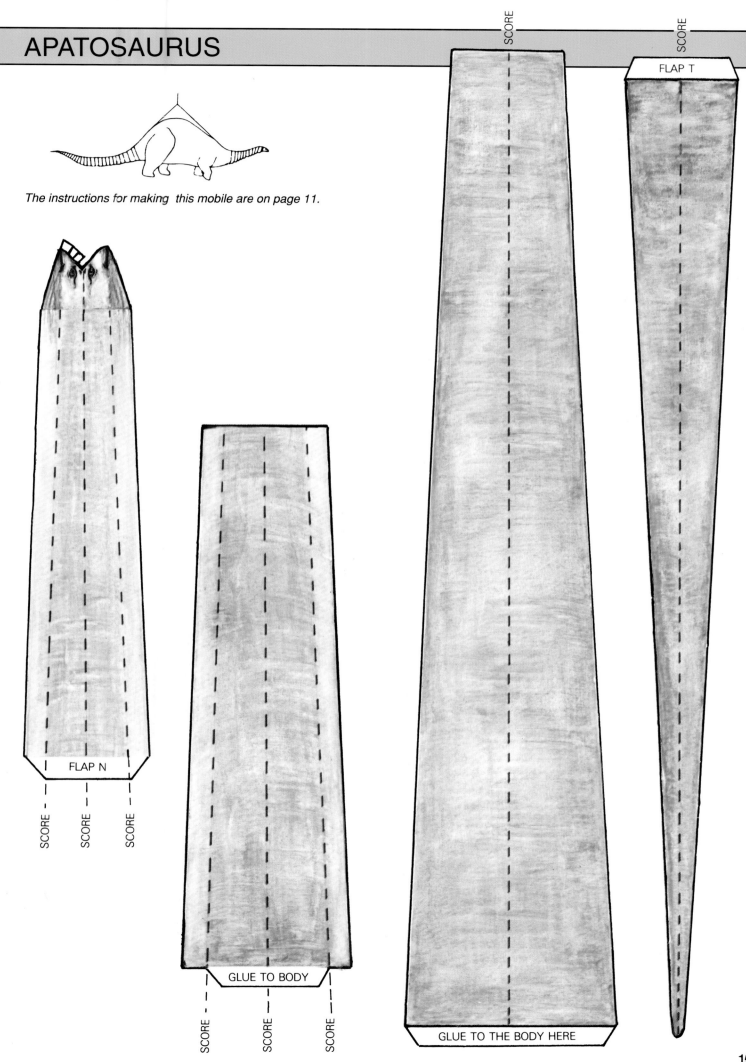

The instructions for making this mobile are on page 11.

FLAP N

SCORE SCORE SCORE

GLUE TO BODY

SCORE SCORE SCORE

SCORE

GLUE TO THE BODY HERE

SCORE

FLAP T

SCORE

15

Despite its ferocious appearance, *Triceratops* was a plant-eating dinosaur. It roamed the plains of North America in large herds about 65 million years ago. It grew up to 11 metres in length and 8.5 tonnes in weight and its head was large in proportion. The two larger horns were up to 1 metre long, but even so were only weapons of defence. With the smaller nose horn they gave it its name, which means 'three horned face'.

For more information see the minibook.

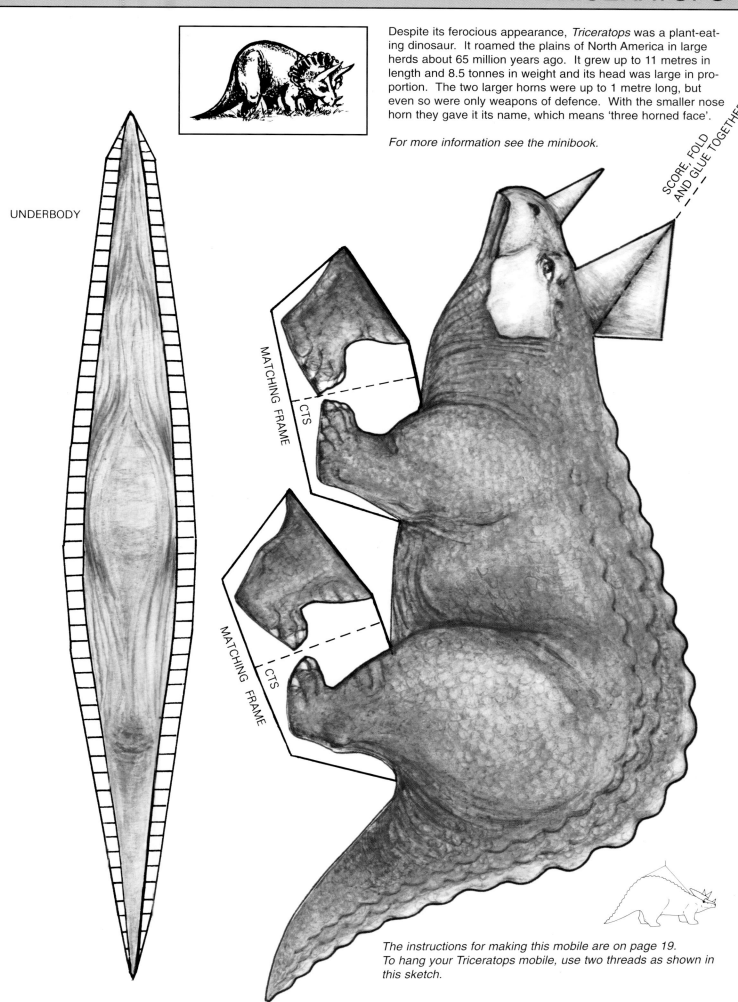

UNDERBODY

MATCHING FRAME

CTS

MATCHING FRAME

CTS

SCORE, FOLD AND GLUE TOGETHER

The instructions for making this mobile are on page 19.
To hang your Triceratops mobile, use two threads as shown in this sketch.

TRICERATOPS

HOW TO MAKE THIS MOBILE

1. Cut out the pieces on this page and on page 17 following the general instructions inside the front cover about scoring, cutting, matching frames and snip-strips.
2. Glue the underbody a few "teeth" at a time to the left side of the body, starting at the chin.
3. Glue the underbody to the right side in the same way.
4. Glue a narrow band along the back, pinching firmly together. The large horns do NOT glue together, but the small one does.
5. Then make the head armour.

Cut the three slots which are marked, and then mould the shape with your fingers so that it looks like the sketch above.

Slide the horns through the slots, pinch the armour over the nose and then use a few spots of glue to hold it in place.

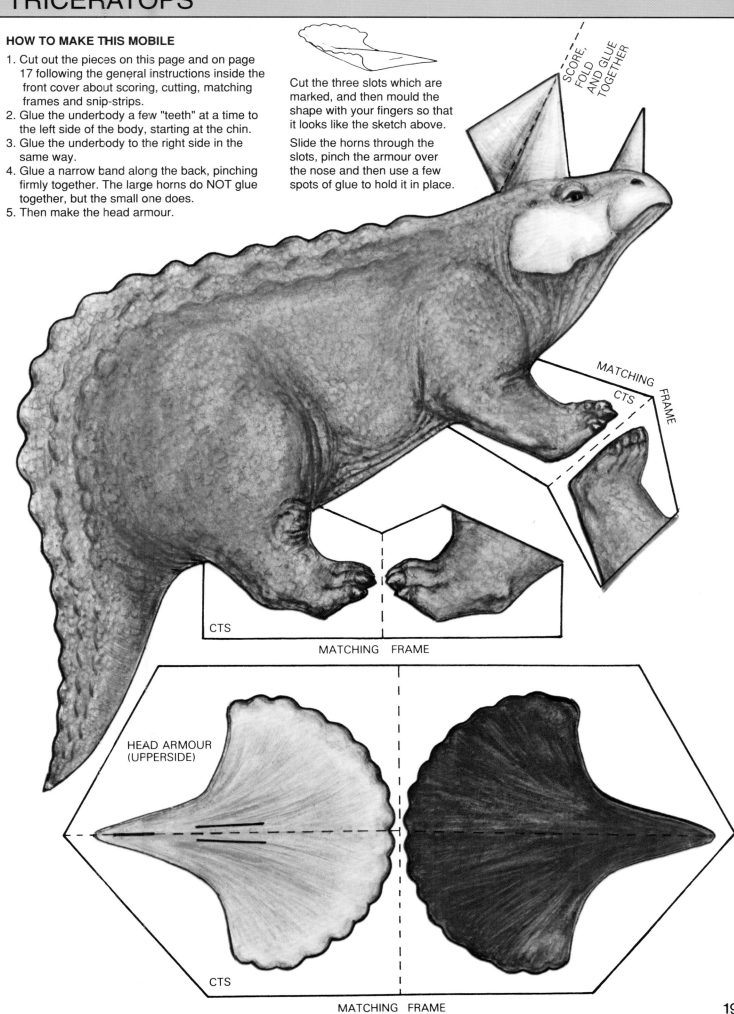

SCORE, FOLD, AND GLUE TOGETHER

MATCHING FRAME

CTS

CTS

MATCHING FRAME

HEAD ARMOUR (UPPERSIDE)

CTS

MATCHING FRAME

an ichthyosaur

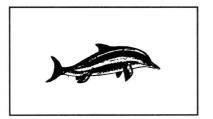

Stenopterygius lived in the warm waters round Western Europe about 175 million years ago. It looked like a present day dolphin and had very similar habits, however it was no relation. We can be sure that *Stenopterygius* looked like this because not only have skeletons been found, but also the impressions of its body outline and skin. It was about 2.5 metres long.

For more information see the minibook.

HOW TO MAKE THIS MOBILE

1. Cut out the pieces on this page, following the general instructions inside the front cover about scoring, cutting, matching frames and snip-strips.
2. Cut the two slots on each side of the body and then insert and glue the flippers in position.
3. Glue the two sides together along the back starting at the nose and glueing a few "teeth" of the snip-strips at a time. The dorsal fin and the tail DO glue together.
4. Press in the flaps on the underside and glue one set over the other. The gaps caused by the curvature are filled by the flaps underneath.
5. Press the flippers slightly outwards.

To hang your Stenopterygius mobile, use a single thread through the dorsal fin, as shown in this sketch.

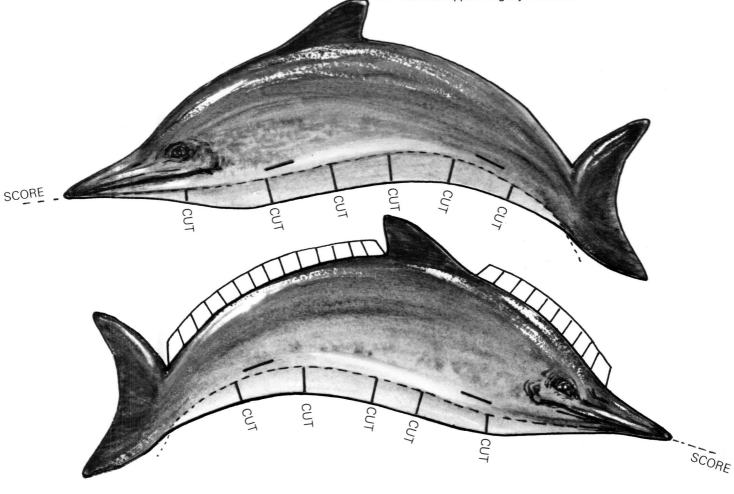

SCORE

CUT CUT CUT CUT CUT CUT

CUT CUT CUT CUT CUT

SCORE

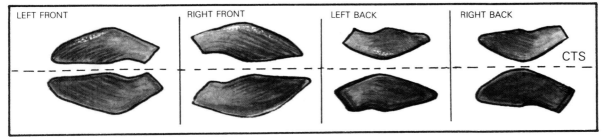

LEFT FRONT	RIGHT FRONT	LEFT BACK	RIGHT BACK

CTS

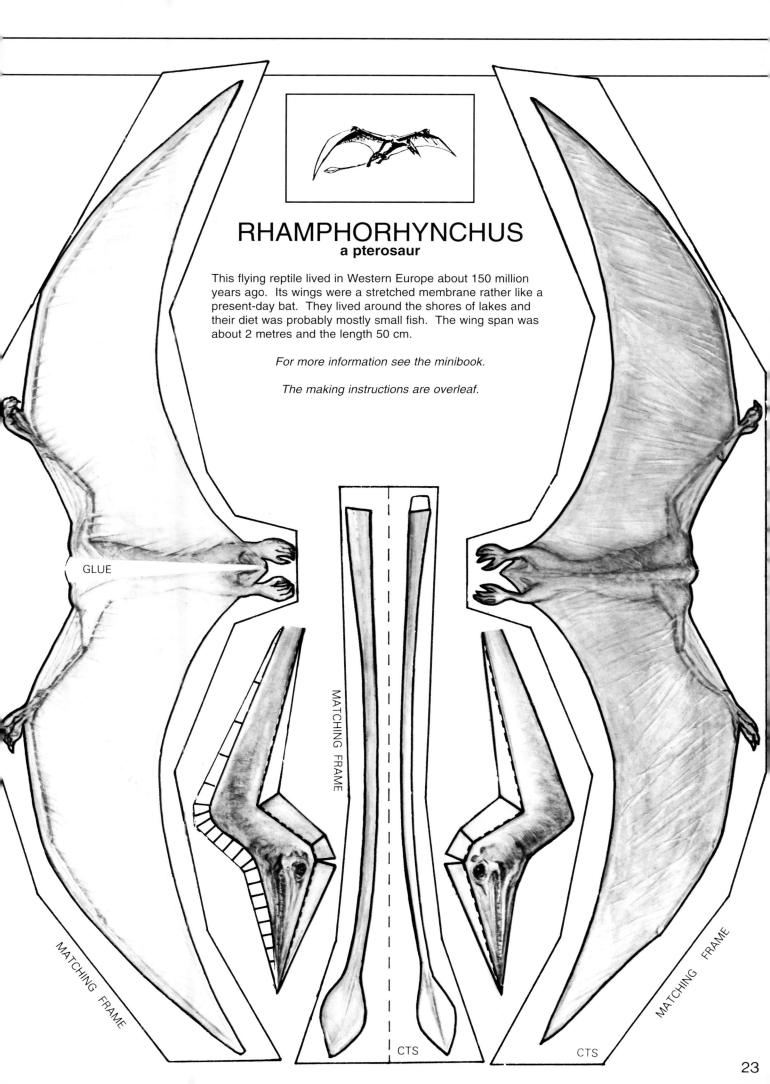

RHAMPHORHYNCHUS
a pterosaur

This flying reptile lived in Western Europe about 150 million years ago. Its wings were a stretched membrane rather like a present-day bat. They lived around the shores of lakes and their diet was probably mostly small fish. The wing span was about 2 metres and the length 50 cm.

For more information see the minibook.

The making instructions are overleaf.

GLUE

MATCHING FRAME

MATCHING FRAME

MATCHING FRAME

MATCHING FRAME

CTS

CTS

To hang your Rhamphorhynchus mobile,
use two threads, as shown in this sketch.

HOW TO MAKE THIS MOBILE

1. Cut out the pieces following the general instructions inside the front cover about scoring, cutting, matching frames and snip-strips. For this mobile the main matching frames are separate but they still glue together back to back before cutting out.
2. Glue the head pieces together using the snip-strips.
3. Glue the tail into position slotting the flap into the body.
4. Bend the larger flaps on top of the head into position so that they overlap and then glue into place.
5. Glue the body into position on the underside of the wings.

Score along ◄────► and then cut out these pages. Instructions for making the minibook are on the inside of the back cover.

DINOSAURS - A LONG STORY

The first dinosaurs lived about 228 million years ago, and for the next 160 million years they were to be found all over the Earth in an astonishing variety of forms, from slow-moving plant-eaters to ferocious quick-moving meat-eaters. There were gigantic dinosaurs which were as heavy as several elephants and others which were scarcely bigger or heavier than rabbits. There were reptiles distantly related to the dinosaurs which lived entirely in the sea and there were other closer relatives which were light enough to fly. The mobiles you have made show just six types out of the hundreds which are known to have existed.

Compare the 160,000,000 year history of the dinosaurs with the 4,000,000 year history of man and the mere 6,000 years which have passed since the dawn of civilisation.

Yet even the long history of the dinosaurs is short compared with the long history of Earth itself.......

1

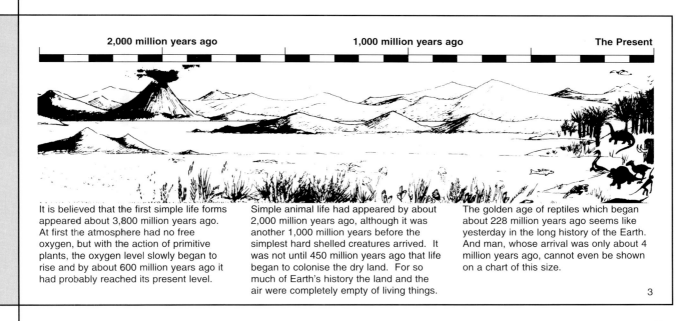

| 2,000 million years ago | 1,000 million years ago | The Present |

It is believed that the first simple life forms appeared about 3,800 million years ago. At first the atmosphere had no free oxygen, but with the action of primitive plants, the oxygen level slowly began to rise and by about 600 million years ago it had probably reached its present level.

Simple animal life had appeared by about 2,000 million years ago, although it was another 1,000 million years before the simplest hard shelled creatures arrived. It was not until 450 million years ago that life began to colonise the dry land. For so much of Earth's history the land and the air were completely empty of living things.

The golden age of reptiles which began about 228 million years ago seems like yesterday in the long history of the Earth. And man, whose arrival was only about 4 million years ago, cannot even be shown on a chart of this size.

3

HOW LONG AGO DID WE KNOW ABOUT DINOSAURS?

Megalosaurus

Curiously, although dinosaurs were on the Earth for a very long time, no-one suspected that they had ever existed until about 1822. A doctor's wife, Mary Mantell, picked up what looked like some large teeth from a pile of road menders' rubble. Her husband became very interested in them and consulted the fossil experts of the time. At first they dismissed the idea that they could be the teeth of a large reptile but gradually more evidence was collected. Dr Mantell named his reptile 'Iguanodon' because it resembled in some way the present day Iguana, although it was very much larger. In the meantime Dean William Buckland of Oxford had named a reptile he had found 'Megalosaurus', which simply means 'big lizard' and that was the first to receive a name - in 1824. The name 'dinosaur' which means 'terrible lizard' was first suggested by Sir Richard Owen and it is often used wrongly or misleadingly to describe any reptile of the dinosaur era. In this book there is also an ichthyosaur (which means 'fishy lizard') and a pterosaur which means 'flying lizard'). However they were reptiles from the dinosaur era, and they do make interesting mobiles!

Iguanodon 5

THE LONG HISTORY OF THE EARTH

4,600 million years ago	4,000 million years ago	3,000 million years ago

The earth was probably formed about 4,600 million years ago from a swirling cloud of dust and gasses. As the core formed, its gravitational force attracted more and more material from space nearby and so it grew and grew to roughly its present size.

This process generated a great deal of heat, so that even the rock melted. However, as time passed it cooled down and the surface solidified. The oldest rocks so far discovered date from about 3,800 million years ago.

The cooling earth was surrounded by hot gasses and steam, but as time passed and they cooled, they gradually condensed and fell as rain - a rain storm that probably lasted 100,000 years!

2

HOW DO WE KNOW WHAT DINOSAURS WERE LIKE?

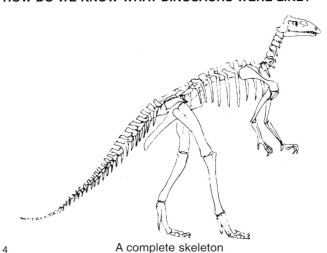

The answer to this is from their fossils which have been found all over the world. Fossils are the bones and shells of creatures which have been 'petrified' while buried in the earth. 'Petrified' means turned to stone, where each molecule of the bone or shell has been replaced by mineral through the action of water in the soil.

Sometimes complete skeletons have been found and then reassembled in museums. Then it is possible to see where the muscles were attached and to build up a picture of the living creature. Further, there are even fossilised footprints, fossilised eggs and fossilised unborn baby dinosaurs so a great deal is known about them.

How do we know what colour they were? The answer is that we do not. The colours chosen for these models are the greens, blues and browns which would camouflage them in their environment. We cannot be sure though that they were not striped like a Zebra or brilliantly coloured like a parrot or a butterfly!

4   A complete skeleton

WHAT WAS THE EARTH LIKE IN THE DINOSAUR ERA?

The earth was very different from today and steadily changed as the continents drifted apart. It was warm all over the whole earth and there were not the marked differences between winter and summer that we see today. The era of the dinosaurs continued through three geological periods, the late Triassic, the Jurassic and the Cretaceous and then ended abruptly. This, and the next three pages give an impression of what it was like then.

LATE TRIASSIC PERIOD

The large landmass began to break up. The climate was very hot and dry and vegetation was sparse except on the margins of swampy rivers and lakes.

JURASSIC PERIOD

The climate gradually changed and became cooler and wetter. The vegetation increased and became more varied.

CRETACEOUS PERIOD

The continents became cooler towards the end of this period and seasons became noticeable as the continents drifted still further apart. Flowering plants and trees developed, some of which we would recognise today.

Score along ←——→ *and then cut out these pages. Instructions for making the minibook are on the inside of the back cover.*

THE LATE TRIASSIC PERIOD (224-208 million years ago)

This drawing of a late Triassic scene shows three of the early dinosaurs
(A) *Plateosaurus*   (B) *Coelophysis*   (C) *Fabrosaurus*
and three other creatures which still exist today in almost unchanged form
(D) Cockroach   (E) Spider   (F) Dragonfly

7

THE CRETACEOUS PERIOD (145-65 million years ago)

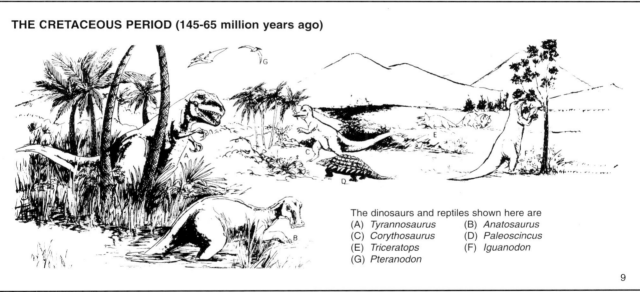

The dinosaurs and reptiles shown here are
(A) *Tyrannosaurus*   (B) *Anatosaurus*
(C) *Corythosaurus*   (D) *Paleoscincus*
(E) *Triceratops*   (F) *Iguanodon*
(G) *Pteranodon*

9

ALLOSAURUS

This flesh-eating dinosaur lived and hunted in North America about 150 million years ago. It reached a length of 10 metres and stood 3 metres high. It was a forerunner by 85 million years of the even larger *Tyrannosaurus rex*.
Allosaurus had three digits on its short front legs, which although armed with sharp claws were probably only used for gripping prey while it was being pulled to pieces by the enormous teeth.

APATOSAURUS

It had small teeth set in a very small head which it used to strip and rake the enormous quantity of plants it needed to eat. It swallowed stones to help break down the plants in its stomach. It had a tiny brain for its size, its height reached 5 metres and with a length of 20 metres and a weight of up to 30 tonnes it was a very large animal indeed. It lived in North America about 150 million years ago.

STENOPTERYGIUS

This ichthyosaur looks very much like a present-day dolphin and its habits were rather similar. However it is no relation. Not only were skeletons of *Stenopterygius* fossilised, but impressions of its body outline and skin were left too, so we can be more certain than with most what it looked like. It lived in the warm seas around Western Europe about 175 million years ago.

11

THE JURASSIC PERIOD (208-145 million years ago)

The dinosaurs and reptiles shown here are
(A) *Ornitholestes*   (B) *Compsognathus*   (C) *Apatosaurus*
(D) *Brachiosaurus*   (E) *Stegosaurus*   (F) *Allosaurus*   (G) *Rhamphorhynchus*

8

THE MOBILES YOU HAVE MADE

TRICERATOPS

The name means 'three horned face' so it is an accurate description of this dinosaur. It grew up to 11 metres long and up to 8.5 tonnes in weight, with its head very large in proportion. The two larger horns were a metre in length but even so were only weapons of defence, for *Triceratops* was a plant-eater, roaming the plains of North America in large herds about 65 million years ago.

10

RHAMPHORHYNCHUS

This pterosaur was about 50cm long and lived in Western Europe about 150 million years ago. Its wings were a stretched membrane between the fourth finger and the body giving a wing span of about 2 metres. The teeth protruded sidewards and forwards so they were used for gripping and holding, not for biting.
They lived around the shores of lakes and their diet was fish and insects.

STEGOSAURUS

This dinosaur is easily recognised by the double row of plates along its back. They could have been a protective armour, but it is more likely they were radiators, allowing the cold blooded creature to gain or lose heat as necessary.
It had small teeth and must have fed on soft plants. In spite of a length of 6 metres and a weight of up to 2 tonnes, its brain was scarcely larger than a walnut.

WHATEVER HAPPENED TO THE DINOSAURS?

About 65 million years ago the fossil record of the dinosaurs all over the world came to an abrupt end. Many theories have been put forward to explain the mystery, but no-one is sure what really happened.
Possibly the change of climate and the onset of cold winters was sufficient to kill off the cold blooded reptiles which had no fur to keep themselves warm. Certainly, it was from that time that the warm blooded mammals with their fur and hair gained the ascendancy which they have maintained to the present day. The meteorite impact of 65 million years ago and a huge outbreak of volcanic activity at the same time may also have played an important role in dinosaur extinction.
Certainly it is true that many other creatures alive in the dinosaur era are still to be seen today, in almost unchanged form - for instance frogs, toads, spiders, sharks, dragonflies and cockroaches to name just a few. It is quite a sobering thought that if the dinosaurs had not died out, we would probably not be here. The mammals had been scurrying around the dinosaurs feet for 160 million years and were able to evolve into all the groups we see today- from horses to man - only after the land became vacant.

Score along ◄──────► and then cut out these pages. Instructions for making the minibook are on the inside of the back cover.

THE LATE TRIASSIC PERIOD (224-208 million years ago)
This drawing of a late Triassic scene shows three of the early dinosaurs
(A) *Plateosaurus*   (B) *Coelophysis*   (C) *Fabrosaurus*
and three other creatures which still exist today in almost unchanged form
(D) Cockroach   (E) Spider   (F) Dragonfly

7

THE CRETACEOUS PERIOD (145-65 million years ago)

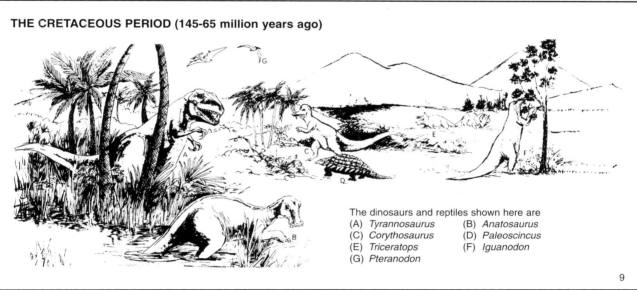

The dinosaurs and reptiles shown here are
(A) *Tyrannosaurus*   (B) *Anatosaurus*
(C) *Corythosaurus*   (D) *Paleoscincus*
(E) *Triceratops*   (F) *Iguanodon*
(G) *Pteranodon*

9

ALLOSAURUS
This flesh-eating dinosaur lived and hunted in North America about 150 million years ago. It reached a length of 10 metres and stood 3 metres high. It was a forerunner by 85 million years of the even larger *Tyrannosaurus rex*.
Allosaurus had three digits on its short front legs, which although armed with sharp claws were probably only used for gripping prey while it was being pulled to pieces by the enormous teeth.

APATOSAURUS
It had small teeth set in a very small head which it used to strip and rake the enormous quantity of plants it needed to eat. It swallowed stones to help break down the plants in its stomach. It had a tiny brain for its size, its height reached 5 metres and with a length of 20 metres and a weight of up to 30 tonnes it was a very large animal indeed. It lived in North America about 150 million years ago.

STENOPTERYGIUS
This ichthyosaur looks very much like a present-day dolphin and its habits were rather similar. However it is no relation. Not only were skeletons of *Stenopterygius* fossilised, but impressions of its body outline and skin were left too, so we can be more certain than with most what it looked like. It lived in the warm seas around Western Europe about 175 million years ago.

11

THE JURASSIC PERIOD (208-145 million years ago)

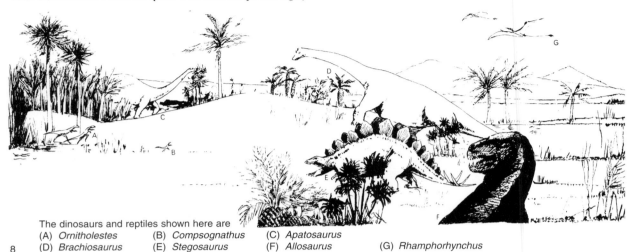

The dinosaurs and reptiles shown here are
(A) *Ornitholestes*   (B) *Compsognathus*   (C) *Apatosaurus*
(D) *Brachiosaurus*   (E) *Stegosaurus*   (F) *Allosaurus*   (G) *Rhamphorhynchus*

THE MOBILES YOU HAVE MADE

TRICERATOPS
The name means 'three horned face' so it is an accurate description of this dinosaur. It grew up to 11 metres long and up to 8.5 tonnes in weight, with its head very large in proportion. The two larger horns were a metre in length but even so were only weapons of defence, for *Triceratops* was a plant-eater, roaming the plains of North America in large herds about 65 million years ago.

RHAMPHORHYNCHUS
This pterosaur was about 50cm long and lived in Western Europe about 150 million years ago. Its wings were a stretched membrane between the fourth finger and the body giving a wing span of about 2 metres. The teeth protruded sideways and forwards so they were used for gripping and holding, not for biting.
They lived around the shores of lakes and their diet was fish and insects.

STEGOSAURUS
This dinosaur is easily recognised by the double row of plates along its back. They could have been a protective armour, but it is more likely they were radiators, allowing the cold blooded creature to gain or lose heat as necessary.
It had small teeth and must have fed on soft plants. In spite of a length of 6 metres and a weight of up to 2 tonnes, its brain was scarcely larger than a walnut.

WHATEVER HAPPENED TO THE DINOSAURS?

About 65 million years ago the fossil record of the dinosaurs all over the world came to an abrupt end. Many theories have been put forward to explain the mystery, but no-one is sure what really happened.
Possibly the change of climate and the onset of cold winters was sufficient to kill off the cold blooded reptiles which had no fur to keep themselves warm. Certainly, it was from that time that the warm blooded mammals with their fur and hair gained the ascendancy which they have maintained to the present day. The meteorite impact of 65 million years ago and a huge outbreak of volcanic activity at the same time may also have played an important role in dinosaur extinction.
Certainly it is true that many other creatures alive in the dinosaur era are still to be seen today, in almost unchanged form - for instance frogs, toads, spiders, sharks, dragonflies and cockroaches to name just a few. It is quite a sobering thought that if the dinosaurs had not died out, we would probably not be here. The mammals had been scurrying around the dinosaurs feet for 160 million years and were able to evolve into all the groups we see today- from horses to man - only after the land became vacant.